Following the Crowd

Following the Crowd

Jaren Partelli

CONTENTS

1

Introduction to Herd Behavior

Definition of Herd Behavior

Herd behavior refers to the phenomenon where individuals in a group make decisions based on the actions or beliefs of others, often leading to a collective behavior that may deviate from individual rationality. This behavior can manifest in various contexts, from financial markets to social media trends, and is driven by psychological factors such as conformity, social influence, and the desire for social acceptance. Understanding herd behavior is essential for psychology students and social media analysts, as it provides insight into why individuals may follow the crowd, sometimes at the expense of their own beliefs or judgments.

One of the key psychological triggers behind herd behavior is the concept of social proof, which suggests that individuals often look to the actions of others to determine the correct course of action, especially in uncertain situations. This reliance on social cues can lead to a phenomenon known as informational social influence, where people assume that the majority's behavior is indicative of the correct behavior. In social media contexts, this can be observed through trends and viral content, where users may engage with or share posts based on their popularity rather than their personal opinion or the validity of the information.

Herd mentality is particularly evident in consumer behavior, where individuals may purchase products or services based on the choices of others rather than their own preferences. This can result in fads or trends that sweep through markets, often fueled by influencers and the visibility of certain items on social media platforms. The psychological underpinnings of this behavior can be attributed to a combination of social identity theory and the desire for belonging, as consumers seek to align themselves with groups that reflect their values or aspirations. Understanding these dynamics is critical for marketers and analysts aiming to leverage herd behavior for brand engagement.

In workplace dynamics, herd behavior can influence decision-making processes and organizational culture. Employees may conform to the opinions or actions of their peers, particularly in environments where a strong group identity exists. This can lead to both positive outcomes, such as enhanced teamwork and collaboration, and negative consequences, such as groupthink, where critical analysis is stifled in favor of consensus. Recognizing the triggers of herd behavior in professional settings can help leaders foster a culture of open dialogue and innovation, allowing for diverse perspectives to thrive.

Cultural influences also play a significant role in shaping herd behavior. Different societies may exhibit varying degrees of collectivism or individualism, affecting how herd mentality manifests across cultures. In educational settings, for example, students may conform to peer behavior due to cultural norms that prioritize group harmony over individual expression. The advent of technology, particularly social media, has further amplified these cultural dynamics by facilitating rapid information sharing and the formation of online communities. By exploring the intersections of culture, technology, and herd behavior, psychology students and analysts can gain a comprehensive understanding of how societal contexts influence individual and group behavior.

Historical Context and Development

The concept of herd behavior has deep historical roots, tracing back to the early observations of social dynamics in human societies. Philosophers and social scientists have long been intrigued by the tendency of individuals to conform to the actions of a larger group, often overriding their personal judgment. From the writings of Aristotle, who discussed the importance of community in shaping individual behavior, to the theories of

Emile Durkheim, who examined collective consciousness, the foundations of herd mentality have been explored through various lenses. These early frameworks set the stage for understanding how social influences can guide decision-making processes, particularly in times of uncertainty.

As societies evolved, so did the manifestations of herd behavior, particularly in response to economic and technological developments. The Industrial Revolution marked a significant turning point, as rapid urbanization led to densely populated cities where individuals were more susceptible to social influences. This period saw the emergence of consumerism, where marketing strategies began to exploit group dynamics. The rise of advertising in the late 19th and early 20th centuries highlighted how emotions and social approval could drive consumer choices, illustrating the psychological triggers that encourage individuals to follow the crowd in pursuit of status or belonging.

With the advent of social media in the 21st century, the dynamics of herd behavior have transformed dramatically. Platforms like Facebook,

Twitter, and Instagram have created new avenues for information dissemination and social interaction, often amplifying herd mentality on an unprecedented scale. The speed at which information spreads online can lead to rapid shifts in public opinion, affecting everything from political movements to consumer trends. Social media not only facilitates the sharing of ideas but also acts as a powerful tool for social validation, where likes and shares can serve as endorsements of behavior, further reinforcing the psychological triggers behind herd behavior.

The impact of herd mentality extends beyond consumer behavior into various domains, including workplace dynamics and educational settings. In professional environments, the pressure to conform can shape organizational culture, influencing everything from decision-making to innovation. The tendency to align with the group can stifle individuality and critical thinking, leading to groupthink, where dissenting opinions are marginalized. In educational contexts, students may exhibit herd behavior in their learning choices, often prioritizing popular opinions or practices over evidence-based approaches, which can stifle creativity and critical analysis.

Culturally, the implications of herd mentality resonate across different societies and communities, often reflecting regional values and social norms. Understanding these cultural dimensions is crucial for psychology students and social media analysts, as it allows for a more nuanced approach to studying herd behavior. Technology, while a facilitator of connection, also poses challenges, as the anonymity and distance it provides can lead to more extreme forms of herd behavior, such as online bullying or radicalization. By examining the historical context and development of herd mentality, we can better comprehend the psychological triggers that drive individuals to conform, ultimately enriching our understanding of human behavior in the modern world.

Importance of Studying Herd Behavior

The study of herd behavior is fundamental to understanding various psychological and social phenomena that shape human interactions and decision-making processes. For psychology students and social media analysts, examining herd behavior provides critical insights into how individuals are influenced by group dynamics. This understanding is essential, as it offers a framework for analyzing collective behaviors in diverse contexts, from consumer trends to workplace dynamics. By recognizing the mechanisms driving herd mentality, these individuals can better navigate and interpret the complex social landscapes in which they operate.

One significant aspect of herd behavior is its manifestation in consumer behavior. Consumers often look to others when making purchasing decisions, and this tendency can lead to trends that reflect collective preferences rather than individual choice. For psychology students, exploring the psychological triggers behind this behavior, such as social proof and conformity, can illuminate why certain products gain popularity. For social media analysts, understanding these triggers is vital for developing effective marketing strategies and predicting market movements based on social media trends and influencer impacts.

In the context of workplace dynamics, herd behavior can influence team cohesion and decision-making processes. Employees may conform to group opinions or behaviors, sometimes at the expense of critical thinking and individual creativity. This phenomenon can lead to both positive outcomes, such as enhanced collaboration, and negative consequences, such as groupthink. By studying herd behavior in educational settings, psychology students can learn how to foster environments that encourage independent thought while also valuing teamwork. Social media analysts can apply these insights to online team dynamics and the influence of virtual interactions on professional relationships.

Cultural contexts also play a crucial role in shaping herd behavior. Different cultures have varying perspectives on conformity and individuality, which can influence how herd mentality manifests in different societies. For instance, collectivist cultures may exhibit stronger herd behaviors compared to individualistic societies, where personal choice is more emphasized. Understanding these cultural impacts enables psychology students to appreciate the nuances of human behavior across different backgrounds. Similarly, social media analysts can tailor their approaches to account for cultural differences in audience behavior and engagement strategies.

Lastly, technology significantly influences herd behavior, especially through social media platforms. The rapid dissemination of information and the ability to connect with large audiences can amplify herd mentality, leading to phenomena such as viral trends or mass movements. For psychology students, examining the psychological implications of technology on herd behavior offers a contemporary lens through which to analyze social influence. For social media analysts, this knowledge is essential for crafting effective campaigns that harness the power of social proof while being mindful of the potential for negative consequences, such as misinformation and online polarization. Overall, the importance of studying herd behavior lies in its ability to enhance our understanding of human psychology and social dynamics, ultimately informing both academic inquiry and practical applications in various fields.

2

Psychological Triggers of Herd Behavior

Social Proof and Conformity

Social proof is a powerful psychological phenomenon that significantly influences behavior, particularly in social contexts. It refers to the tendency of individuals to look to the actions and behaviors of others to guide their own decisions, especially in ambiguous situations. This concept is deeply rooted in the idea of conformity, where individuals feel compelled to align their behaviors with those of a larger group. In the realm of social psychology, social proof serves as a critical mechanism for understanding how group dynamics can shape individual choices and lead to herd behavior.

In the context of social media, the impact of social proof is magnified. Platforms like Facebook, Twitter, and Instagram create environments where individuals are constantly exposed to the actions and opinions of others. When users see a large number of likes, shares, or positive comments on a particular post, they may feel compelled to align their views or behaviors accordingly. This phenomenon is particularly evident in consumer behavior, where trends can rapidly emerge as users imitate the purchasing decisions of others. The immediacy and visibility of social media amplify the effects of social proof, leading to swift shifts in public opinion and consumer choices.

The influence of social proof extends beyond consumer behavior into workplace dynamics. Organizational cultures often reflect herd mentality, where employees conform to the prevailing attitudes and behaviors of their peers. This conformity can stifle individuality and creativity, as team members may hesitate to voice dissenting opinions or propose innovative ideas that diverge from the norm. Understanding this dynamic is crucial for leaders aiming to foster a more open and collaborative work environment. Encouraging diverse viewpoints and recognizing individual contributions can mitigate the negative impacts of social proof in professional settings.

Cultural factors also play a significant role in shaping the degree to which individuals conform to social proof. Different societies may have varying thresholds for conformity based on cultural norms and values. For instance, collectivist cultures may encourage a stronger reliance on social proof, leading to heightened herd behavior, while individualistic cultures might promote more independent decision-making. This cultural lens is essential for comprehending how social proof manifests in various contexts, from educational settings to broader societal trends.

Technology further complicates the dynamics of social proof and conformity. The rapid evolution of digital communication has transformed how individuals interact and share information, creating new avenues for herd behavior to flourish.

Algorithms that prioritize popular content can create echo chambers, reinforcing existing beliefs and behaviors among users. As psychology students and social media analysts, it is vital to critically examine these technological influences and their implications for social behavior. By understanding the interplay between social proof, conformity, and technology, we can better navigate the complexities of herd mentality in contemporary society.

Fear of Missing Out (FOMO)

Fear of Missing Out (FOMO) is a psychological phenomenon that has gained significant attention in recent years, particularly in the context of social media and consumer behavior. FOMO refers to the anxiety that arises from the belief that others might be having rewarding experiences from which one is absent. This feeling often leads individuals to seek out opportunities to participate in social gatherings, purchase trending products, or engage in popular activities, driven by the desire to not feel excluded. The prevalence of FOMO in today's hyper-connected digital landscape can be linked to the rise of social media platforms, which serve as constant reminders of what others are doing, enhancing feelings of inadequacy and social comparison.

In the realm of herd mentality, FOMO plays a crucial role in influencing group behavior. When individuals perceive that a significant number of people are engaging in a particular behavior or trend, they are more likely to conform to that behavior themselves, driven by the fear of being left out. This dynamic is particularly evident in consumer behavior, where trends can spread rapidly through social media channels. The desire to belong and be part of a collective experience often overrides personal preferences, leading individuals to make choices based on what is popular rather than what is genuinely desired. This behavior not only reinforces the herd mentality but also perpetuates a cycle of consumption that is heavily influenced by social validation.

The impact of FOMO is not limited to consumer choices; it also extends to workplace dynamics. Employees may feel pressured to partake in social activities or initiatives that they may not be genuinely interested in, simply to avoid being perceived as disengaged or out of the loop. This phenomenon can lead to an unhealthy work environment where individuals prioritize social acceptance over their own values and interests. Consequently, organizations may witness a decline in genuine collaboration and innovation, as employees conform to group norms out of fear rather than motivation. Understanding how FOMO influences workplace behavior is essential for fostering a culture that values individual contributions while still encouraging team cohesion.

Culturally, FOMO can vary significantly across different societies and social groups. In cultures that emphasize collectivism, the fear of exclusion may be more pronounced, as social belonging is a critical aspect of identity. Conversely, in more individualistic cultures, the manifestation of FOMO might be tied to personal achievement and competition. These cultural nuances can influence how individuals respond to social pressures and the extent to which they allow FOMO to dictate their choices. Educators and social scientists must consider these cultural differences when studying herd behavior, particularly in educational settings where peer influence is a powerful factor in student engagement and participation.

Finally, technology plays a pivotal role in amplifying the effects of FOMO. The instant gratification provided by social media platforms allows users to witness real-time experiences of others, which can exacerbate feelings of inadequacy and urgency to join in. This constant exposure to curated highlights of others' lives can create a distorted perception of reality, leading individuals to chase after experiences that they believe will validate their worth or social status. As psychology students and social media analysts explore the intersection of technology and human behavior, understanding the mechanisms behind FOMO becomes essential. By addressing the psychological triggers that fuel FOMO, strategies can be developed to mitigate its negative impacts and promote healthier engagement with social influences.

Authority and Influence

Authority and influence play crucial roles in understanding herd behavior, particularly as they interact with social dynamics within various contexts such as consumer behavior, workplace environments, and educational settings. The psychological principle of authority suggests that individuals are more likely to conform to behaviors and beliefs endorsed by perceived leaders or experts. This phenomenon can be observed in numerous scenarios, from following a celebrity's product endorsement on social media to adhering to the directives of a supervisor in a workplace. The weight given to authority figures can amplify the effects of herd mentality, leading individuals to align with group behaviors even when they may personally disagree.

In the realm of social media, the influence of authority figures becomes particularly pronounced. Influencers, often regarded as modern-day authorities, wield significant power over their followers' opinions and actions. Their endorsements can create a ripple effect that encourages herd behavior, particularly in consumer markets.

For instance, when a popular influencer promotes a product, their large following may feel compelled to adopt similar purchasing behaviors, often disregarding their own preferences. This dynamic showcases how authority in social media can distort individual decision-making processes, leading to widespread conformity based on perceived popularity rather than personal choice.

Cultural factors also play a critical role in shaping how authority and influence manifest in herd behavior. Different cultures have varying degrees of respect for authority, which can impact the extent to which individuals conform to group norms. In collectivist cultures, for example, there may be a stronger inclination to follow authoritative figures, reinforcing herd behavior. Conversely, in more individualistic societies, people may be more inclined to resist authority, potentially leading to a different expression of herd mentality. Understanding these cultural nuances is essential for social media analysts and psychologists alike, as they navigate how authority influences group behavior across diverse populations.

Workplace dynamics serve as an illustrative case of authority and influence in action. Employees often look to their managers for guidance and validation of their actions. When leaders endorse specific behaviors or decisions, these can quickly become norms within the workplace, fostering an environment where individuals feel pressured to conform. This can lead to both positive outcomes, such as increased teamwork, and negative consequences, such as groupthink, where critical thinking is sacrificed for the sake of conformity. The balance of authority and influence in such settings is crucial, as it can dictate the overall health of organizational culture and employee satisfaction.

Educational environments present yet another context in which authority and influence shape herd behavior. Teachers and administrators often hold significant sway over students' attitudes and actions. Their authority can guide students toward desired behaviors, such as academic integrity or participation in school activities. However, the influence of peers can also challenge this authority, leading to complex dynamics where students may feel torn between following the crowd and adhering to authoritative guidance. Educators must be aware of these psychological triggers to foster an environment that encourages healthy individual expression while still promoting collective goals. Understanding the interplay of authority and influence is essential for effectively addressing herd behavior in educational settings.

3

Herd Mentality in Consumer Behavior

Group Decision Making

Group decision-making is a fundamental aspect of human interaction, particularly relevant in understanding herd behavior. In psychology, group dynamics play a crucial role in how decisions are made, as individuals often look to the collective for cues on how to act. This reliance on group consensus can lead to both beneficial outcomes and detrimental consequences, illustrating the duality of herd mentality. The psychological mechanisms underpinning group decision-making include social validation, conformity, and the diffusion of responsibility, all of which can significantly influence the choices made within a group context.

One significant factor in group decision-making is the phenomenon of social validation, where individuals seek assurance that their opinions align with those of the majority. This desire for acceptance can lead to conformity, as people may suppress their own preferences or beliefs to align with the group. Social media platforms exacerbate this tendency, as the visibility of group opinions and behaviors can create a pressure to conform, further entrenching herd mentality. In online environments, where likes and shares serve as indicators of social approval, the impact of social validation on decision-making processes becomes even more pronounced, prompting individuals to prioritize collective sentiment over personal judgment.

The diffusion of responsibility is another critical element influencing group decision-making. In a group context, individuals often perceive that the responsibility for outcomes is shared among all members, leading to a reduction in personal accountability. This can be particularly evident in workplace dynamics, where employees may defer decision-making to others or rely on group consensus to justify their choices. While this can foster collaboration and collective problem-solving, it can also result in poor decisions if the group becomes overly influenced by dominant voices or fails to critically evaluate options, demonstrating how herd behavior can manifest in professional settings.

Cultural factors also play a vital role in shaping group decision-making processes. Different cultures exhibit varying levels of collectivism and individualism, which directly influence how decisions are approached within groups. In collectivist societies, for instance, the emphasis on group harmony and consensus can lead to stronger herd behavior, as individuals prioritize the group's welfare over personal opinions. Conversely, in more individualistic cultures, there may be a greater tendency to assert personal viewpoints, potentially leading to conflict within the group. Understanding these cultural impacts is essential for social media analysts and psychologists to navigate and predict group behavior in diverse contexts.

Finally, the rise of technology has transformed the landscape of group decision-making. Digital platforms facilitate instantaneous communication and information sharing, amplifying the effects of herd behavior. Decisions can be influenced by trends that rapidly spread across social media, creating a sense of urgency that may override rational consideration. Educational settings also reflect this shift, as students increasingly look to their peers for guidance, often leading to a collective mindset that can stifle individual critical thinking. As technology continues to shape how groups interact, it is imperative for psychology students and professionals to examine the interplay between technological advancements and the psychological triggers that drive herd behavior, ensuring a comprehensive understanding of group decision-making in the modern world.

Brand Loyalty and Social Influence

Brand loyalty is a fundamental aspect of consumer behavior, deeply influenced by social dynamics and psychological triggers. In the context of herd mentality, individuals often look to their peers when making purchasing decisions, leading to a phenomenon where people are more likely to choose brands that are popular within their social circles. This alignment with group preferences not only fosters a sense of belonging but also reinforces brand loyalty, as consumers become emotionally attached to the brands endorsed by their peers. The interplay between social influence and brand loyalty highlights the importance of understanding the psychological mechanisms that drive these behaviors.

Social media plays a pivotal role in shaping brand loyalty through its ability to amplify social influence. Platforms such as Instagram, Twitter, and Facebook create environments where individuals are constantly exposed to their peers' preferences and endorsements. Influencers and trendsetters can significantly sway public opinion, causing a ripple effect that encourages others to adopt similar brand loyalties. This is particularly relevant in today's digital age, where the immediacy and reach of social media can turn a niche brand into a household name overnight. The visibility of brand choices made by friends and acquaintances on social media platforms can trigger a herd mentality, as users seek to align themselves with what they perceive to be popular or desirable.

The psychological triggers behind herd behavior in brand loyalty are multifaceted. One key factor is the desire for social validation; consumers often feel pressured to conform to the preferences of their peers to avoid social exclusion. This need for acceptance can lead individuals to prioritize brands that are widely favored, even if they personally prefer alternatives. Additionally, the bandwagon effect, a cognitive bias where the perceived popularity of a choice influences individual preferences, plays a significant role in driving brand loyalty. As more people choose a particular brand, others may follow suit, reinforcing the cycle of loyalty and conformity.

In workplace dynamics, herd mentality can manifest in employee preferences for certain brands that are popular among colleagues or industry leaders. This phenomenon can influence purchasing decisions for office supplies, technology, and even services that are considered the industry standard. Employees may feel compelled to align their choices with those of their peers, fostering a culture of conformity that can hinder diversity in brand selection. Understanding this dynamic can help organizations cultivate an environment that values individual preferences while recognizing the impact of social influence on brand loyalty.

Culturally, the impact of herd mentality on brand loyalty can vary significantly. In collectivist societies, where group cohesion and conformity are prized, brand loyalty may be more pronounced as individuals seek to reflect their community's values. Conversely, in more individualistic cultures, brand choices may be more influenced by personal preferences, though social influence still plays a critical role. Educators and analysts in the field of psychology and social media can leverage these insights to better understand consumer behavior and the factors that contribute to brand loyalty in different contexts. By recognizing the intricate relationship between social influence and brand loyalty, stakeholders can develop strategies that effectively engage consumers and foster long-term loyalty.

Case Studies of Successful Herd Marketing

Case studies of successful herd marketing provide valuable insights into the dynamics of herd behavior and its implications for consumer decision-making. One prominent example is the launch of the iPhone by Apple. The initial release in 2007 generated immense buzz and anticipation, largely driven by the company's ability to create a sense of exclusivity and urgency. Apple's strategy involved not only innovative product design but also a carefully crafted marketing campaign that played on social proof. The sight of long lines outside Apple stores, filled with eager customers, reinforced the perception that the iPhone was a must-have item, leading many others to join the queue. This phenomenon exemplifies how crowd behavior can significantly influence individual purchasing decisions, demonstrating the power of herd mentality in consumer behavior.

Another noteworthy case is the viral success of the ALS Ice Bucket Challenge in 2014. This social media campaign not only raised awareness about amyotrophic lateral sclerosis (ALS) but also generated substantial fundraising for research. The challenge involved people pouring a bucket of ice water over their heads and nominating others to do the same, creating a ripple effect across platforms like Facebook and Twitter. The campaign's success can be attributed to its ability to tap into social influence and the psychological triggers associated with herd behavior. As more individuals participated, the desire to conform and be part of a collective movement led to an exponential increase in participation, highlighting how social media can amplify herd mentality and drive collective action.

The case of "Black Friday" shopping events further illustrates herd marketing's effectiveness. Retailers often employ strategies that create a sense of urgency and exclusivity, such as limited-time offers and doorbuster deals. The phenomenon of consumers camping out overnight to secure the best deals exemplifies the power of herd behavior, as individuals are motivated not only by the desire for discounts but also by the social dynamics at play. The sheer visibility of crowds and the anticipation of shared experiences can significantly enhance the appeal of participating in such events. This case underscores how environmental cues and social pressures can lead to herd behavior in consumer contexts, influencing purchasing decisions on a massive scale.

In workplace dynamics, the implementation of open office spaces serves as a compelling example of herd marketing principles. Many companies have adopted this trend under the assumption that it fosters collaboration and innovation. However, the decision to adopt such layouts often stems from a desire to align with perceived best practices in the industry. As organizations observe competitors moving toward open spaces, they may feel compelled to follow suit, driven by herd mentality. This phenomenon can result in a collective shift in workplace culture, impacting employee satisfaction and productivity. Understanding the psychological triggers behind this behavior can provide insights into the broader implications of herd mentality in organizational settings.

Finally, the impact of technology on herd behavior is exemplified by the phenomenon of social media influencers. Brands increasingly collaborate with influencers to leverage their substantial online followings, creating a sense of trust and credibility that encourages consumers to adopt similar behaviors. The success of these marketing strategies is rooted in the psychological principles of social proof and conformity; when individuals see their peers or admired figures endorsing a product, they are more likely to follow suit. This case highlights the evolving landscape of herd marketing in the digital age, where technology not only facilitates the spread of information but also amplifies the psychological triggers that drive herd behavior in consumer markets.

4

Social Media Influence on Herd Mentality

The Role of Social Media Platforms

Social media platforms have become pivotal in shaping contemporary herd behavior, acting as conduits for information dissemination and social interaction. These platforms facilitate rapid communication that can influence the opinions and actions of large groups of individuals. The inherent design of social media encourages users to engage with content that resonates with their social circles, reinforcing shared beliefs and behaviors. This phenomenon is particularly relevant in understanding how collective decision-making is influenced by online interactions, as individuals often look to their peers for validation and cues, thus perpetuating herd mentality.

The design of social media inherently promotes the visibility of popular opinions and trends, which can create a bandwagon effect. When a particular idea, product, or behavior gains traction on these platforms, users may feel compelled to join in, even if it contradicts their initial beliefs or preferences. This effect is magnified by algorithms that prioritize trending content, ensuring that popular posts reach a wider audience. As a result, the visibility of certain behaviors or opinions can skew perceptions of what is normative, leading individuals to conform to the prevailing sentiments of the crowd, often without critically evaluating the information presented.

Moreover, social media serves as a breeding ground for social proof, where individuals look to the actions of others as a benchmark for their own behavior. This psychological trigger is especially potent in consumer behavior, where online reviews, likes, and shares can significantly influence purchasing decisions. The ability to observe others engaging with a product or idea can create a sense of urgency or desirability, prompting individuals to align their actions with the collective. In workplaces, similar dynamics can occur as employees observe their peers' behaviors on social media, leading to conformity in workplace culture and dynamics.

Cultural factors also play a significant role in shaping how social media influences herd mentality. Different cultural backgrounds can affect how individuals interpret social cues and the extent to which they feel pressure to conform. For example, collectivist cultures may experience stronger herd behavior on social media, as aligning with group norms is often emphasized. In educational settings, this cultural influence can manifest in group projects or discussions where students may feel compelled to go along with the majority view, diminishing individual critical thinking and creativity.

Lastly, the impact of technology on herd mentality extends beyond mere interaction; it also involves the analysis of data generated through social media. Social media analysts can examine trends and patterns of behavior, providing insights into how information spreads and influences group dynamics. Understanding these mechanisms is crucial for both psychological research and practical applications in fields such as marketing and organizational behavior. By analyzing the role of social media platforms in fostering herd mentality, students can gain valuable insights into the psychological triggers that underlie collective behavior and the implications for society at large.

Viral Trends and Their Impact

Viral trends have become a defining characteristic of the social media landscape, significantly influencing behavior across various domains. These trends, often characterized by rapid spread and widespread participation, serve as a compelling example of herd mentality in action. Individuals, motivated by a desire for social validation or belonging, often engage with these trends, leading to collective behaviors that transcend individual rationality. Understanding the psychological triggers that catalyze these trends is vital for both psychology students and social media analysts who seek to comprehend the mechanics of social influence.

One major psychological trigger behind viral trends is the principle of social proof. When individuals observe others engaging in a particular behavior, they often interpret this as an indication of its appropriateness or desirability. This phenomenon is especially pronounced in online environments, where visibility and engagement metrics can amplify the perceived popularity of a trend. As users witness their peers participating in viral challenges or adopting specific hashtags, they may feel compelled to join in, reinforcing the trend's momentum and further contributing to the herd behavior.

Moreover, the role of emotional contagion in viral trends cannot be overlooked. Content that elicits strong emotional responses—whether humor, awe, or even outrage—tends to spread more rapidly than neutral content. This emotional engagement acts as a catalyst for sharing, encouraging users to not only participate in the trend but also to amplify it within their networks. In educational settings, for instance, teachers may leverage viral trends to engage students, tapping into their existing interests while fostering a collective learning experience that aligns with the social dynamics observed in digital spaces.

The impact of viral trends extends beyond individual behaviors to influence consumer behavior and workplace dynamics. In consumer markets, products or brands that are associated with viral trends often experience a surge in demand, driven by the herd mentality. This phenomenon illustrates how social media can create a feedback loop, where the popularity of a product is bolstered by its viral status, further entrenching consumer behavior patterns. Similarly, in workplace environments, viral trends can shape team dynamics and organizational culture, as employees may align their behaviors with trending norms to foster a sense of belonging or to gain social capital.

Culturally, viral trends can serve as a lens through which to examine broader societal attitudes and values. They often reflect current events, social issues, or shifts in public sentiment, providing insight into the collective psyche of a population. As trends emerge and dissipate, they can reveal underlying cultural narratives and highlight the influence of technology on contemporary social behavior. In this context, psychology students and social media analysts are uniquely positioned to dissect the implications of these trends, offering valuable insights into the mechanisms of herd mentality and its profound effects on individual and collective behavior in a rapidly evolving digital world.

Analyzing Online Communities

Analyzing online communities provides valuable insights into the dynamics of herd behavior in the digital age. These communities are characterized by their ability to facilitate rapid information exchange, enabling individuals to connect over shared interests and beliefs. This interconnectedness can amplify collective opinions, driving groupthink and influencing individual decision-making. For psychology students and social media analysts, understanding the mechanisms behind these online interactions is crucial for deciphering how and why individuals conform to group norms, especially in contexts where behavioral cues can lead to significant societal shifts.

The psychological triggers that underpin herd behavior in online communities often stem from social validation and the desire for acceptance. Users may feel compelled to align their opinions with the dominant views expressed within these spaces, leading to conformity that can overshadow personal beliefs. This phenomenon is particularly pronounced in platforms where likes, shares, and comments serve as metrics of approval. As individuals observe others endorsing a particular stance or product, they may experience pressure to conform, driven by the fear of social ostracism or the perceived need to belong. This dynamic highlights the importance of social influence in shaping consumer behavior and community engagement.

Moreover, the role of anonymity in online communities can further complicate the analysis of herd behavior. While anonymity can empower individuals to express themselves without fear of judgment, it can also lead to a disinhibition effect, where people are more likely to engage in behaviors they might avoid in face-to-face interactions. This can foster a more extreme version of herd mentality, as individuals may be emboldened to participate in or propagate controversial opinions and actions. Understanding the balance between anonymity and accountability is essential for social media analysts who seek to comprehend the implications of online discourse on group behavior.

Cultural factors significantly influence how herd behavior manifests within online communities. Different cultures may prioritize collectivism or individualism, which can shape how individuals engage with their peers. In collectivist societies, for instance, the pressure to conform may be stronger, leading to more pronounced herd behavior. Conversely, in individualistic cultures, there may be greater resistance to conformity, which can manifest as a counter-movement within online spaces. Analyzing these cultural dimensions helps in identifying patterns of behavior and the contextual factors that contribute to the emergence of herd mentality in various online environments.

In educational settings, the implications of herd behavior are particularly noteworthy. Online communities in educational contexts can foster collaboration and collective learning; however, they can also perpetuate misinformation or reinforce biases if left unchecked. Understanding the psychological triggers behind these dynamics equips educators and analysts with the tools to create healthier online learning environments. By fostering critical thinking and encouraging diversity of thought, educators can mitigate the negative effects of herd behavior while promoting a more inclusive and constructive dialogue among students.

5

Herd Mentality in Workplace Dynamics

Team Cohesion and Groupthink

Team cohesion refers to the degree to which team members work together effectively towards a common goal, fostering an environment of trust, collaboration, and mutual support. In the context of group dynamics, high levels of team cohesion can enhance productivity, creativity, and employee satisfaction. However, this cohesion can also lead to groupthink, a psychological phenomenon where the desire for harmony and conformity within a group results in irrational decision-making. Understanding the balance between healthy team cohesion and the detrimental effects of groupthink is crucial for both psychology students and social media analysts, especially when examining how these dynamics manifest in various environments, including workplaces and online communities.

Groupthink typically arises in teams characterized by strong cohesion, where members prioritize consensus over critical evaluation. This often leads to the suppression of dissenting opinions and a lack of consideration for alternative viewpoints. The consequences of groupthink can be severe, resulting in flawed decisions that overlook potential risks or innovative solutions. In a social media context, this behavior can be amplified as users often engage with content that aligns with their group's norms, leading to echo chambers where dissenting voices are marginalized. Analyzing these patterns helps understand how social media influences herd mentality and contributes to the reinforcement of groupthink in digital interactions.

The interplay between team cohesion and groupthink is particularly pronounced in consumer behavior, where brands leverage social proof to create a sense of belonging among their audience. When consumers observe that others are purchasing a product or endorsing a brand, they may feel compelled to conform to the group's choices, frequently without critically assessing the product's merits. This phenomenon illustrates how herd mentality can shape buying decisions, as individuals prioritize group consensus over personal preferences. Social media platforms facilitate this dynamic by providing a constant stream of peer endorsements, thus blurring the line between individual choice and collective behavior.

In workplace dynamics, the tension between cohesion and groupthink can present challenges to organizational effectiveness. Leaders must cultivate an environment where team members feel empowered to express divergent opinions and challenge the status quo. Encouraging open dialogue and fostering psychological safety are essential strategies to minimize the risks of groupthink while maintaining cohesion. Training programs that focus on critical thinking and group decision-making can equip teams with the skills necessary to navigate these complexities, promoting a culture where innovation thrives without sacrificing unity.

Culturally, the impacts of herd mentality on team cohesion and groupthink can vary significantly across different societies. Some cultures may emphasize collectivism, where group harmony is prioritized, potentially increasing the likelihood of groupthink. In contrast, individualistic cultures might encourage debate and dissent, thereby reducing the incidence of groupthink. As psychology students and social media analysts explore these cultural dimensions, they gain deeper insight into how collective behaviors are shaped by social norms and technological influences. This understanding is essential for analyzing herd behavior in educational settings, workplaces, and beyond, providing a comprehensive perspective on the psychological triggers that underpin our social interactions.

Leadership and Herd Behavior

Leadership plays a pivotal role in shaping herd behavior, significantly influencing how individuals conform to group dynamics. Leaders, whether in a corporate setting, social movement, or online community, often serve as focal points for the collective mindset. Their ability to inspire, motivate, and direct followers can either encourage independent thought or foster conformity. In environments where leaders exhibit strong charisma and decisiveness, followers may feel compelled to align with the leader's vision, often at the expense of their own judgment. This phenomenon can be particularly pronounced in educational settings, where teachers and administrators wield significant influence over student behavior and attitudes, potentially amplifying herd mentality.

The relationship between leadership and herd behavior is further complicated by the social media landscape. Influencers and public figures can rapidly sway public opinion, often leading to widespread adoption of certain behaviors, attitudes, or trends. Social media platforms facilitate this dynamic by creating echo chambers where popular opinions are amplified and dissenting views marginalized. For psychology students and social media analysts, understanding the mechanisms of influence is crucial. They must analyze how leaders within social media can create a perception of consensus, prompting users to adopt behaviors and beliefs simply because they appear to be widely accepted, thereby reinforcing the herd mentality.

Psychological triggers such as authority, social proof, and scarcity play significant roles in this context. Leaders often exploit these triggers to galvanize followers, effectively manipulating the psychological underpinnings of herd behavior. For example, when a respected leader endorses a product or idea, followers are likely to perceive it as more credible. Similarly, the sense of urgency created by limited-time offers can lead consumers to act impulsively, driven by the fear of missing out. Understanding these triggers allows psychology students and analysts to dissect the strategies employed by leaders to foster herd behavior and its implications for consumer behavior and workplace dynamics.

In workplace environments, effective leadership can either mitigate or exacerbate herd behavior. Leaders who promote a culture of open dialogue and critical thinking encourage employees to voice their opinions and challenge the status quo. In contrast, authoritarian leadership styles can suppress individual expression, leading to conformity and groupthink. This dynamic can significantly affect organizational culture and productivity. Educational institutions can benefit from fostering environments where students and faculty feel empowered to express diverse viewpoints, thereby reducing the likelihood of herd behavior stemming from leadership influence.

Cultural factors also play a crucial role in the intersection of leadership and herd behavior. Different cultures have varying norms regarding conformity and individualism, which can affect how leadership is perceived and followed. In collectivist cultures, for example, leaders may be more effective at mobilizing groups, as the societal emphasis on harmony and group cohesion resonates with followers. Conversely, in more individualistic cultures, followers might resist herd behavior when it conflicts with personal beliefs or values. Understanding these cultural dimensions is essential for psychology students and social media analysts as they explore the complexities of herd behavior and its implications across different contexts.

Consequences of Herd Mentality in Organizations

Herd mentality, the phenomenon where individuals conform to the behaviors or beliefs of a group, can have significant consequences within organizations. One of the most immediate impacts of this behavior is the suppression of individual creativity and critical thinking. When employees prioritize group consensus over their unique perspectives, innovative ideas are often stifled. This cultural dynamic can lead to a homogenized workplace where risk-averse attitudes prevail, ultimately hindering the organization's ability to adapt to market changes or embrace new technologies. In environments where conformity is rewarded, the potential for groundbreaking solutions dimin-

ishes, leaving organizations vulnerable to stagna-
tion.

In addition to hindering creativity, herd mentality can lead to poor decision-making processes
in organizations. When groups prioritize consensus, they may overlook critical information or fail
to consider alternative viewpoints. This groupthink phenomenon can result in significant mis-
calculations, as decisions become based on the
prevailing sentiments rather than a comprehensive
analysis of facts. Such errors are particularly pronounced in high-stakes situations, such as financial
investments or strategic planning, where the consequences of misguided decisions can be cata-
strophic. The tendency to follow the crowd may
also result in a lack of accountability, as individuals
feel less responsible for decisions made collectively.

Social media exacerbates the consequences of
herd mentality in organizations by amplifying
group dynamics. The instantaneous nature of information dissemination allows for rapid shifts in
public perception, often driven by trending opinions rather than grounded evidence. Employees
may feel pressured to align with popular opinions

or emerging trends on social platforms, particularly when these views are shared by influential figures within or outside the organization. This phenomenon can create an echo chamber effect, where dissenting opinions are marginalized, and the organization risks adopting a superficial understanding of complex issues. The allure of social validation can further entrench herd behavior, leading to decisions that prioritize image over substance.

Cultural impacts also play a critical role in shaping herd mentality within organizations. Organizations that cultivate a culture of conformity may inadvertently promote an environment where dissent is discouraged. In such settings, employees might hesitate to voice concerns or propose alternative approaches, thereby reinforcing the cycle of herd behavior. This can be particularly detrimental in multicultural organizations, where diverse perspectives are essential for innovation and effective problem-solving. Emphasizing cultural sensitivity and inclusivity is crucial in mitigating the negative consequences of herd mentality and fostering a healthy dialogue among employees.

Finally, the consequences of herd mentality can extend to employee morale and organizational trust. When individuals feel compelled to conform rather than express their authentic selves, it can lead to disengagement and dissatisfaction. A culture that prioritizes conformity over individuality may foster resentment and a sense of alienation among employees, ultimately affecting productivity and retention rates. Organizations must recognize the importance of encouraging diverse viewpoints and creating an environment where individuals feel safe to express dissent. By doing so, they can mitigate the adverse effects of herd mentality and cultivate a dynamic, innovative workplace that thrives on collaboration and open discourse.

6

Cultural Impacts of Herd Mentality

Cultural Norms and Group Behavior

Cultural norms play a pivotal role in shaping group behavior, acting as unspoken guidelines that dictate acceptable actions, beliefs, and attitudes within a community. These norms are often rooted in historical traditions, societal values, and collective experiences, which influence how individuals within a group interact with one another. Understanding these norms is crucial for psychology students and social media analysts alike, as they provide insight into the mechanisms that drive herd behavior. When individuals conform to group norms, they often do so to belong, avoid conflict, or gain social approval, leading to a phenomenon where personal beliefs may be overshadowed by the collective mindset.

The influence of cultural norms is particularly pronounced in the context of social media, where platforms serve as amplifiers of group behavior. Social media not only facilitates the rapid dissemination of information but also reinforces existing cultural norms through likes, shares, and comments. This creates an environment where individuals are more likely to align their opinions and behaviors with those of the majority, further entrenching herd mentality. For social media analysts, recognizing how cultural norms manifest online is essential in understanding trends, viral content, and the psychological triggers that lead users to conform to group behaviors, sometimes at the expense of their individual judgment.

In consumer behavior, cultural norms significantly impact purchasing decisions and brand loyalty. Marketers often capitalize on herd mentality by leveraging social proof, where the actions of others influence an individual's choices. For instance, a product that is widely endorsed or purchased by a group can create a sense of urgency or desirability, prompting others to follow suit. This phenomenon underscores the importance of cultural context; what is deemed popular or acceptable in one culture may not hold the same significance in another. Psychology students must analyze these dynamics critically, considering how cultural influences shape consumer behavior and the ethical implications of manipulating these triggers.

Workplace dynamics also reveal the power of cultural norms and their contribution to herd behavior. In professional settings, organizational culture can dictate how employees interact, share ideas, and make decisions. A strong culture may foster collaboration and innovation, while a toxic environment could stifle individuality and promote conformity. Understanding these cultural influences is vital for fostering healthy workplace dynamics, as leaders and managers can implement strategies that encourage diverse perspectives and mitigate the negative effects of herd mentality. By addressing these cultural aspects, organizations can create a more inclusive atmosphere that values individual contributions while still benefiting from the advantages of group cohesion.

Finally, the impact of technology on cultural norms cannot be overlooked, as it continuously reshapes how individuals engage with one another. The rise of digital communication tools has altered traditional means of interaction, leading to new cultural practices that influence group behavior. This shift presents both opportunities and challenges for educators and psychologists alike. In educational settings, for instance, technology can enhance collaboration but may also promote conformity through digital platforms that prioritize popular opinions over critical thinking. As students navigate these new cultural landscapes, understanding the interplay between technology and cultural norms will be essential in fostering environments that encourage independent thought while recognizing the inherent human tendency to follow the crowd.

Collective Identity and Social Movements

Collective identity serves as a crucial underpinning for social movements, shaping the motivations and actions of individuals within a group. This concept refers to the shared sense of belonging and the common characteristics that individuals perceive as defining their group. In the context of social movements, collective identity fosters solidarity and a unified purpose among participants, which can amplify their collective voice and increase the likelihood of effecting social change. Understanding how collective identity is formed and maintained can provide valuable insights into the dynamics of herd behavior, particularly in how groups mobilize around shared goals and values.

The role of social media in shaping collective identity cannot be overstated. Platforms such as Facebook, Twitter, and Instagram serve as vital tools for individuals to connect, share experiences, and disseminate information related to social causes. These platforms facilitate the rapid spread of ideas and narratives, enabling individuals to identify with broader movements that resonate with their own experiences. As people engage with content that aligns with their beliefs, social media creates echo chambers that reinforce collective identity, making participants more likely to join and contribute to social movements. This phenomenon highlights the intersection of herd mentality and social media, illustrating how digital environments can amplify collective sentiments and mobilize action.

Psychological triggers play a significant role in shaping collective identity within social movements. Emotions such as anger, hope, and empathy can act as catalysts that drive individuals to participate in collective action. The urgency and intensity of these emotions often heighten the sense of belonging to a group, reinforcing an individual's commitment to the cause. Furthermore, group dynamics, including social validation and conformity, can lead to a heightened sense of identity among participants. As individuals observe their peers engaging in activism, they are more likely to align their behaviors and attitudes with the group, further solidifying their collective identity and enhancing herd behavior.

In consumer behavior, collective identity influences purchasing decisions and brand loyalty. When consumers identify with a brand or product that embodies their values, they are more inclined to engage in behaviors that support it, often driven by the desire to be part of a larger community. This collective identity can lead to herd behavior, where individuals make purchasing choices based on group norms rather than personal preference. Marketers often leverage this phenomenon by creating campaigns that emphasize community and belonging, effectively tapping into the psychological triggers that drive herd mentality in consumer settings.

Educational settings also reflect the dynamics of collective identity and herd behavior. Students often form groups based on shared interests, beliefs, or backgrounds, creating environments where peer influence is prevalent. In these contexts, students may adopt certain attitudes or behaviors to align with their peers, which can impact their academic performance and social interactions. Understanding the role of collective identity in education can inform strategies to promote inclusive environments that celebrate diversity while minimizing the negative aspects of herd behavior, such as groupthink or exclusionary practices. By fostering a positive collective identity, educators can empower students to engage critically with their peers and the broader societal issues at hand.

Regional Differences in Herd Behavior

Regional differences in herd behavior can be attributed to various cultural, social, and economic factors that shape how individuals respond to group dynamics. In different geographical locations, the values and norms prevalent within a culture influence the extent to which people conform to group behavior. For instance, collectivist societies, such as those found in many parts of Asia, often demonstrate a higher tendency toward herd behavior compared to individualistic societies in the West. This divergence can be traced back to the foundational beliefs about community and individualism, with collectivist cultures emphasizing harmony and conformity, while individualistic cultures prioritize personal choice and independence.

Social media plays a crucial role in amplifying herd behavior across regions, but its impact is often moderated by local contexts. In regions where social media penetration is high, trends can spread rapidly, leading to significant shifts in consumer behavior and public opinion. However, the nature of these shifts can vary. For instance, in urbanized areas with diverse populations, social media may facilitate a blending of ideas and a more eclectic approach to trends, while in more homogeneous rural areas, herd behavior may reinforce existing norms and values. Understanding these regional nuances is essential for social media analysts who seek to predict trends and behaviors within specific demographics.

The psychological triggers that underlie herd behavior can also differ significantly by region. In some cultures, the desire for social approval and belonging may drive individuals to conform more readily to group norms. In contrast, in regions with a strong emphasis on independence, psychological triggers may lean more toward a fear of exclusion from the group rather than a desire for acceptance. Educational settings often reflect these regional differences, where students from collectivist cultures may exhibit a greater tendency to follow peers, while those from individualistic backgrounds might prioritize personal judgment, leading to varying classroom dynamics and group interactions.

Economic factors further complicate the landscape of herd behavior across different regions. In economically developing areas, the influence of herd mentality may manifest more prominently in consumer behavior, as individuals often rely on the behaviors of others to inform their purchasing decisions. Conversely, in economically advanced regions, consumers may be more aware of marketing strategies and brand identities, leading to a more discerning approach to consumption. This divergence illustrates how economic stability or instability can shape the psychological triggers that drive herd behavior within different contexts.

Lastly, technology's impact on herd mentality can vary significantly across regions, influenced by both access to technology and the types of platforms that dominate in specific locales. In regions with advanced technological infrastructure, the rapid spread of information can lead to swift changes in public sentiment and behavior. However, in areas with limited access to technology, traditional forms of communication may still hold sway, leading to a slower diffusion of trends and ideas. Understanding these regional differences is vital for those studying herd behavior, as it provides insight into how cultural, social, and technological contexts shape the complex interplay between individual psychology and group dynamics.

7

Educational Settings
and Herd Behavior

Peer Influence in Academic Settings

Peer influence in academic settings plays a pivotal role in shaping students' attitudes, behaviors, and overall academic performance. The presence of peers can significantly impact engagement levels, motivation, and even the choices students make regarding their educational paths. This influence often manifests through various social dynamics, as students tend to align their behaviors with those of their peers, whether consciously or subconsciously. Understanding these dynamics is essential for educators and psychologists alike, as it sheds light on how peer interactions can foster both positive and negative academic outcomes.

Research has shown that peer pressure can lead to increased motivation among students, particularly in collaborative environments. When students perceive that their peers are striving for high academic standards, they are more likely to adopt similar attitudes. This phenomenon is often observed in study groups, where the collective effort encourages individual accountability and academic diligence. Conversely, negative peer influences can also emerge, particularly in settings where academic dishonesty or disengagement is prevalent. In such cases, students may feel compelled to conform to behaviors that undermine their academic integrity, highlighting the dual-edged nature of peer influence.

The rise of social media has further complicated the dynamics of peer influence in educational settings. Platforms such as Facebook, Instagram, and TikTok provide students with a constant stream of information about their peers' achievements and social activities. This visibility can amplify the effects of peer influence, as students often compare themselves to their online peers. The pressure to maintain a certain image or achieve similar academic success can lead to heightened anxiety and stress. Understanding how social media shapes these perceptions is crucial for recognizing the broader implications for student well-being and academic performance.

Cultural factors also play a significant role in how peer influence manifests in educational contexts. Different cultures prioritize various values and behaviors, which can affect how students interact with their peers. In collectivist cultures, for instance, group harmony and consensus may be emphasized, leading to a stronger alignment with group norms. In contrast, individualistic cultures may promote personal achievement, resulting in competitive behaviors among students. These cultural differences can significantly influence how peer pressure is experienced and managed within academic environments, affecting both group dynamics and individual outcomes.

Ultimately, addressing peer influence in academic settings requires a nuanced understanding of the psychological triggers behind herd behavior.

Educators and psychologists must recognize the complex interplay between peer dynamics, social media, and cultural contexts. By fostering environments that encourage positive peer interactions and promoting individual accountability, it is possible to harness the benefits of peer influence while mitigating its negative consequences. Engaging students in discussions about peer dynamics and providing them with tools to navigate social pressures can empower them to make informed decisions about their academic journeys.

Group Projects and Collaborative Learning

Group projects and collaborative learning represent a quintessential model for understanding how herd behavior manifests in educational environments. In academic settings, students often engage in teamwork to achieve shared goals, which is a microcosm of broader social dynamics. The interactions that occur within these groups can reflect psychological triggers that underlie herd behavior, such as conformity, social validation, and the desire for acceptance. When students work to-gether, they not only share knowledge but also in-fluence one another's perceptions and actions, fostering a collective mindset that can either en-hance or hinder learning outcomes.

The dynamics of group projects can be heavily influenced by social media, which serves as a plat-form for collaboration and communication. In an age where digital interactions often precede face-to-face exchanges, the influence of social media on group identity becomes pronounced. Students may rely on platforms like group chats or social networks to coordinate efforts, leading to the for-mation of norms that dictate group behavior. This interconnectedness can amplify herd mentality, as individuals may be swayed by the opinions and ac-tions of their peers shared online, resulting in a col-lective behavior that prioritizes group consensus over individual critical thinking.

Moreover, collaborative learning environments can also highlight the psychological triggers behind herd behavior. The presence of a dominant group member can create a social hierarchy that influ-ences decision-making processes. Those who are more reticent may conform to the opinions of louder voices, reflecting a common psychological phenomenon where individuals prefer to align with perceived authority figures within a group. This can stifle creativity and independent thought, illustrating how herd mentality can become detrimental to the educational experience when conformity overshadows individual contributions.

Furthermore, the cultural context in which group projects occur can significantly impact how herd behavior is expressed. Different cultural backgrounds bring varying expectations regarding teamwork, communication styles, and authority dynamics. In cultures that emphasize collectivism, for example, students may be more inclined to prioritize group harmony over personal opinions, leading to a stronger adherence to herd behavior. Conversely, in more individualistic cultures, there may be a greater emphasis on personal contributions, potentially mitigating the effects of herd mentality. Understanding these cultural nuances is crucial for educators aiming to foster effective collaborative learning experiences.

In conclusion, the exploration of group projects and collaborative learning through the lens of herd behavior provides valuable insights for psychology students and social media analysts alike. By examining how psychological triggers influence group dynamics, the role of social media in shaping collective attitudes, and the cultural implications of teamwork, we can better understand the complexities of herd mentality in educational settings. This understanding not only informs pedagogical strategies but also equips students with the tools to navigate and analyze social behaviors both within and beyond the classroom, ultimately enhancing their academic and professional endeavors.

Strategies to Mitigate Negative Herd Behavior

To mitigate the effects of negative herd behavior, it is essential to first understand the psychological triggers that often lead individuals to conform to group actions, particularly in environments influenced by social media and technology. One effective strategy involves fostering critical thinking skills among individuals. Educational institutions and organizations can implement training programs that encourage questioning norms and evaluating information critically. By teaching students and employees to analyze situations independently, it empowers them to resist blind conformity and make informed decisions based on evidence rather than peer pressure or groupthink.

Another strategy is the promotion of diverse perspectives within groups. Encouraging a culture that values dissenting opinions can help counteract the tendency toward herd behavior. This can be achieved through structured brainstorming sessions and open forums where individuals feel safe expressing differing views. In workplaces, for instance, creating interdisciplinary teams can lead to richer discussions and innovative solutions, as team members bring unique experiences and viewpoints. This diversity not only enriches the decision-making process but also diminishes the likelihood that individuals will simply follow the crowd without consideration of alternative paths.

Social media analysts play a crucial role in identifying and addressing the dynamics of herd behavior in digital spaces. By leveraging analytics tools, they can monitor trends and discern patterns that indicate rising herd mentality. Implementing real-time feedback mechanisms can also help users recognize when they are being influenced by collective behavior. For example, platforms could incorporate features that highlight divergent opinions or provide statistics on varying viewpoints, thereby nudging users to reflect before conforming to the prevailing sentiment. This kind of transparency can help mitigate impulsive decision-making driven by herd mentality.

In educational settings, implementing programs that focus on emotional intelligence is another effective strategy. By enhancing self-awareness and empathy, students can better understand their motivations and the influences of those around them. Workshops and role-playing exercises can help students develop skills to navigate social pressures and recognize when they might be succumbing to herd behavior. Additionally, incorporating discussions about the psychological underpinnings of herd mentality in the curriculum can empower students to identify these behaviors in themselves and others, fostering a more reflective approach to group dynamics.

Lastly, engaging technology responsibly is vital in mitigating the negative impacts of herd behavior. Organizations and educators should advocate for responsible use of social media, emphasizing the importance of verifying information before sharing it. Providing guidelines on digital literacy can equip individuals with the tools necessary to discern credible sources from misinformation. By cultivating a more discerning digital culture, stakeholders can reduce the propensity for panic-driven herd behavior, particularly in situations where rapid dissemination of information can lead to collective irrationality. Overall, these strategies create a more resilient mindset capable of resisting the allure of negative herd behavior.

8

Technology's Impact
on Herd Mentality

Algorithms and Behavioral Predictions

Algorithms play a crucial role in shaping behavioral predictions, particularly in the context of social media and its influence on herd mentality. These algorithms analyze vast amounts of data to identify patterns in user behavior, preferences, and interactions. By utilizing machine learning techniques, they can predict how individuals might respond to certain stimuli, such as trending topics or viral content. This predictive capability is not only instrumental for social media platforms in tailoring user experiences but also serves as a catalyst for herd behavior, whereby individuals are more likely to conform to the actions and opinions of others due to the perceived popularity or credibility of a trend.

The influence of algorithms extends beyond mere content recommendation; they also create feedback loops that reinforce certain behaviors. For instance, when a post gains traction, the algorithm prioritizes it, leading to increased visibility and engagement. This phenomenon can create a snowball effect, where users are drawn to popular content, often without critical evaluation. The psychological triggers that drive herd behavior, such as social proof and conformity, become amplified in these environments, as individuals may feel compelled to align with the majority to avoid social exclusion or to enhance their social standing.

Moreover, the design of these algorithms often reflects and exacerbates existing societal biases. For example, if an algorithm is trained on data that reflects particular cultural norms or consumer behaviors, it may inadvertently prioritize content that aligns with those norms while sidelining alternative viewpoints. This selective amplification can perpetuate stereotypes and reinforce existing herd mentalities within specific demographic groups. As a result, understanding the interplay between algorithms and behavioral predictions is essential for psychologists and social media analysts who seek to comprehend the broader implications of social media influence on herd behavior.

In workplace dynamics, algorithms can impact group decision-making processes. When collective behavior is driven by data-driven insights, employees may rely on algorithmic recommendations to guide their actions. This reliance can foster a herd mentality, where individuals may prioritize algorithmically derived consensus over independent thought. The psychological triggers associated with herd behavior, such as the desire for acceptance and fear of dissent, can lead to conformity in professional settings, potentially stifling innovation and critical analysis. Recognizing these dynamics is vital for fostering a culture that encourages diverse perspectives and constructive dissent.

Finally, the educational sector faces unique challenges and opportunities regarding algorithm-driven behavioral predictions. As students increasingly engage with digital learning platforms, the algorithms that personalize educational content can influence their learning trajectories and peer interactions. The potential for herd behavior to manifest in educational settings is significant, as students may gravitate toward popular opinions or trends, affecting their academic choices and social interactions. Educators must be aware of these dynamics to cultivate an environment where critical thinking and individual expression are valued alongside the natural inclination toward social conformity. Understanding these principles will enable future psychologists and social media analysts to navigate and influence the complex landscape of herd behavior effectively.

The Role of Artificial Intelligence

The integration of artificial intelligence (AI) into the analysis of herd behavior marks a significant advancement in our understanding of social dynamics. In the context of psychology and social media, AI has the capacity to process vast amounts of data, identifying patterns and trends that may not be immediately observable to human analysts. This capability allows researchers and practitioners to explore how psychological triggers influence herd behavior across various domains, including consumer behavior and workplace dynamics. By leveraging AI, we can gain insights into the mechanisms that drive individuals to conform to the behaviors and opinions of others, often without conscious awareness.

AI algorithms can analyze social media interactions to uncover the psychological underpinnings of herd mentality. For instance, sentiment analysis tools can assess the emotional tone of posts and comments, revealing how collective emotions can sway individual decisions. This understanding is crucial for social media analysts, as it enables them to predict and influence trends. By recognizing the factors that contribute to herd behavior, businesses can tailor their marketing strategies, crafting messages that resonate with the collective sentiments of their target audience. Thus, AI becomes a powerful ally in deciphering the complex interplay between social influence and individual decision-making.

In educational settings, AI's role extends to identifying how herd behavior manifests among students. By analyzing engagement patterns and participation levels in digital learning environments, AI can help educators recognize when students are conforming to peer behaviors, whether positively or negatively. For example, an AI system might highlight when students tend to adopt certain opinions or behaviors based on the dominant views expressed in online discussions. This awareness can inform teaching strategies, encouraging educators to foster critical thinking and independent decision-making, thereby mitigating the adverse effects of herd mentality in academic contexts.

Moreover, the cultural implications of herd mentality in the digital age cannot be overlooked. AI tools can analyze cultural narratives and social norms as they evolve on social media platforms. By examining how different cultures respond to collective behavior, researchers can identify overarching themes that influence herd mentality across diverse groups. This cross-cultural analysis is essential for understanding the global landscape of social influence, allowing psychologists to tailor interventions and educational programs that account for cultural differences in herd behavior.

Finally, the intersection of AI and herd mentality presents ethical considerations that must be addressed. As AI systems become more adept at influencing behavior, we must question the consequences of deploying these technologies for manipulation or control. The potential for AI to exploit psychological triggers raises concerns about autonomy and informed decision-making. For psychology students and social media analysts, it is imperative to engage critically with these tools, ensuring that their application enhances understanding and promotes positive outcomes rather than exacerbating the negative aspects of herd behavior. Navigating this complex landscape will be vital for shaping the future of social influence in a responsible manner.

Future Trends in Technology and Herd Behavior

The intersection of technology and herd behavior has become a focal point for understanding how social dynamics are evolving in the digital age. As technology continues to advance, its influence on collective behavior, particularly in the context of social media, is increasingly profound. Psychology students and social media analysts must recognize that the tools and platforms designed for communication can significantly amplify herd mentality. The algorithms that govern social media platforms often prioritize content that resonates with popular sentiment, thereby creating echo chambers. These echo chambers reinforce existing beliefs and behaviors, leading to a more pronounced herd mentality as individuals seek validation from their peers.

In the realm of consumer behavior, future trends suggest that technology will further entrench herd dynamics. Online shopping platforms increasingly utilize social proof mechanisms, such as reviews, ratings, and trending products, to guide consumer choices. As these platforms become more sophisticated, they will likely leverage advanced data analytics and artificial intelligence to predict and influence purchasing behaviors. Consumers may find themselves more susceptible to herd behavior as personalized recommendations and targeted advertisements create a sense of urgency and desirability around products that are perceived as popular or trending. This shift raises important questions about autonomy and decision-making in consumer contexts.

Workplace dynamics are also poised for transformation through technological advancements. Remote work tools and collaborative platforms can either mitigate or exacerbate herd behavior in organizational settings. On the one hand, these technologies can facilitate open communication and diverse opinions, potentially leading to more democratic decision-making processes. On the other hand, they can reinforce conformity, as individuals may feel pressured to align with prevailing opinions in virtual discussions. As organizations increasingly rely on technology for team interactions, understanding the psychological triggers that drive herd behavior will be essential for fostering a healthy workplace culture.

Cultural impacts of herd mentality in the context of technology cannot be overlooked. As global connectivity increases, cultural exchanges become more frequent, leading to the rapid spread of ideas and behaviors across borders. This cultural diffusion can enhance herd behavior, as individuals adopt trends from different cultures without fully understanding their context. Educational settings are particularly susceptible to these influences, where students may emulate behaviors observed in their peers or through online interactions. The role of educators will evolve as they seek to counteract negative herd influences while promoting critical thinking and individual decision-making skills.

Looking ahead, it is crucial for psychology students and social media analysts to remain vigilant about the implications of technology on herd behavior. Ongoing research should focus on identifying the psychological triggers that drive collective decision-making in increasingly complex technological environments. As technology continues to shape social dynamics, understanding these trends will be vital for developing strategies that promote healthy social interactions. By examining the interplay between technological advancements and herd mentality, professionals in psychology and social media can contribute to more informed and responsible use of these powerful tools, ultimately fostering environments that prioritize individual agency within collective contexts.

9

Strategies to Manage Herd Behavior

Individual Awareness and Decision Making

Individual awareness plays a pivotal role in decision-making processes, particularly when considering the influence of herd behavior. Understanding how personal cognition interacts with social pressures can illuminate why individuals sometimes conform to group norms, even when those norms contradict their own beliefs or preferences. This subchapter delves into the psychological mechanisms that drive individual awareness and its critical interplay with herd mentality, highlighting the nuances of decision-making in various contexts.

At the core of individual awareness is the concept of self-awareness, which refers to an individual's ability to recognize their own thoughts, feelings, and motivations. This self-recognition is essential for making informed decisions, especially in group settings. When individuals are attuned to their internal states, they are more likely to assess the validity of external influences. However, in environments saturated with social cues—such as workplaces or social media platforms—individuals often experience cognitive overload, leading them to rely on heuristics rather than deliberate thought. As a result, the potential for herd behavior increases, as decisions become less about personal conviction and more about alignment with perceived group consensus.

The influence of social media significantly amplifies the effects of herd mentality on individual decision-making. Platforms designed for rapid information sharing create an environment where trends can emerge and spread instantaneously, often overshadowing individual judgment. Users may find themselves swayed by popular opinions or viral phenomena, sometimes without critical evaluation. This phenomenon is exacerbated by the psychological triggers of social validation and fear of missing out, which can lead individuals to prioritize collective acceptance over personal beliefs. Consequently, understanding these dynamics is crucial for psychology students and social media analysts who seek to dissect the factors that contribute to herd behavior in digital contexts.

Cultural factors also play a significant role in shaping individual awareness and its impact on decision-making. Different cultures have varying degrees of collectivism and individualism, which influence how decisions are made within groups. In collectivist cultures, the pressure to conform can be particularly strong, as individuals may prioritize group harmony over personal preferences. Conversely, in more individualistic societies, there may be greater emphasis on personal opinion, potentially leading to resistance against herd behavior. Education about these cultural influences is essential for understanding how individuals navigate decision-making in diverse environments, as it allows for a deeper exploration of the factors that either facilitate or impede individual awareness.

Finally, the implications of individual awareness in decision-making extend into various domains, including consumer behavior and workplace dynamics. In consumer settings, awareness of personal values and beliefs can empower individuals to make choices that align with their identity, rather than simply following trends. Similarly, in workplace environments, promoting a culture of awareness and critical thinking can reduce the likelihood of detrimental herd behavior, fostering innovation and diverse perspectives. By fostering individual awareness, educators and leaders can cultivate environments that encourage thoughtful decision-making, ultimately mitigating the adverse effects of herd mentality and enhancing overall group dynamics.

Educating on Psychological Triggers

Understanding psychological triggers is essential for grasping the mechanisms behind herd behavior. Psychological triggers are stimuli that provoke emotional responses, influencing decisions and actions. In the context of herd behavior, these triggers can manifest in various ways, including fear, social proof, and conformity. For psychology students and social media analysts, recognizing these triggers is crucial for analyzing how individuals make choices in social settings, especially when influenced by group dynamics and peer behaviors.

One of the primary psychological triggers is social proof, which refers to the tendency to look to others for cues on how to behave. This phenomenon is particularly evident in consumer behavior, where individuals often rely on the actions and opinions of others to guide their purchases. In social media, platforms amplify this effect through likes, shares, and comments, leading users to conform to popular opinions or trends. Understanding this trigger can help analysts predict consumer reactions and design marketing strategies that leverage collective behaviors.

Fear is another potent psychological trigger that can drive herd behavior. In uncertain situations, individuals often look to the group for reassurance, leading to collective decision-making based on fear rather than rational thought. This dynamic is prevalent in workplace environments, where anxiety about job security or organizational changes can lead to a group consensus that may not necessarily align with individual interests. Educating on this trigger can assist students and professionals in recognizing when fear may be influencing group dynamics and decision-making processes.

Cultural impacts also play a significant role in shaping psychological triggers related to herd behavior. Different cultures have varying thresholds for conformity and individualism, which can affect how triggers manifest in group settings. For example, collectivist cultures may prioritize group harmony and consensus, making individuals more susceptible to herd behavior. In contrast, individualistic cultures might encourage personal expression, leading to resistance against group pressures. Understanding these cultural nuances is vital for psychology students and analysts working in diverse contexts, as it allows for a more nuanced interpretation of herd dynamics.

Technological advancements have further complicated the landscape of psychological triggers. The omnipresence of social media has created new channels through which information spreads rapidly, often amplifying herd behavior. The immediacy of online interactions can exacerbate emotional responses, making users more likely to react impulsively to trends or crises. Educating on the intersection of technology and psychological triggers is essential for understanding contemporary herd behavior, particularly in educational settings where students are increasingly influenced by digital interactions. By fostering awareness of these triggers, students and analysts can better navigate and influence herd dynamics in various environments.

Policy Recommendations for Organizations

Organizations looking to mitigate the adverse effects of herd behavior while harnessing its potential for positive outcomes should consider a multifaceted approach. First and foremost, it is essential to establish an environment that encourages critical thinking and individual decision-making. This can be achieved through training programs designed to enhance analytical skills and promote open discussions. By integrating exercises that challenge prevailing assumptions and encourage diverse viewpoints, organizations can empower their members to question popular narratives rather than blindly following them.

In the realm of social media influence, organizations must develop strategies that promote responsible consumption of information. This involves educating employees and consumers alike about the psychological triggers behind herd behavior, particularly in digital spaces. Workshops that focus on recognizing cognitive biases, such as confirmation bias and social proof, can help individuals become more discerning regarding the content they encounter online. Furthermore, organizations should consider implementing guidelines for social media engagement that emphasize the importance of verifying sources and critically assessing the motivations behind trending topics.

Consumer behavior is significantly influenced by herd mentality, and organizations must navigate this landscape with care. To do so, they should engage in market research that identifies the factors driving herd behavior within their target demographic. This research can inform marketing strategies that leverage social proof while also promoting authenticity and transparency. By showcasing genuine testimonials and fostering a community-based approach, organizations can cultivate trust and mitigate the risks associated with blind conformity among consumers.

In workplace dynamics, it is crucial for organizations to foster a culture of inclusivity and psychological safety. Leaders should encourage employees to voice dissenting opinions and reward innovative thinking, even when it deviates from the norm. Regular feedback sessions and team-building activities can enhance interpersonal relationships and reduce the tendency for groupthink. Additionally, organizations should be vigilant about recognizing the signs of herd behavior, such as sudden shifts in team morale or decision-making processes, and intervene proactively to address any issues that arise.

Lastly, organizations should consider the cultural impacts of herd mentality in their policy recommendations. Understanding the unique cultural contexts in which they operate can help organizations design interventions that resonate with their members. This may involve collaborating with cultural experts or incorporating insights from social psychology to tailor programs that reflect the values and norms of their audience. By embracing a culturally aware approach, organizations can better navigate the complexities of herd behavior and leverage its dynamics for constructive outcomes.

10

Conclusion

Summary of Key Findings

The exploration of herd behavior reveals a complex interplay of psychological triggers that shape individual actions within group contexts. One of the key findings is that social influence significantly impacts decision-making processes. Individuals often rely on the actions of others as a heuristic to navigate uncertainty, leading to a tendency to conform to group norms. This reliance is particularly pronounced in ambiguous situations where personal knowledge is limited, illustrating how social validation can drive collective behavior. In various contexts, from consumer choices to workplace dynamics, this phenomenon underscores the importance of understanding the conditions that foster herd mentality.

In the realm of social media, findings indicate that platforms serve as amplifiers of herd behavior. The instant connectivity and visibility of actions taken by others create an environment where individuals are constantly exposed to social cues. This exposure not only normalizes certain behaviors but also escalates the urgency to conform due to the fear of missing out or being left behind. The rapid spread of trends and collective actions online exemplifies how digital environments can enhance the psychological triggers of herd behavior, presenting both opportunities and challenges for social media analysts aiming to decipher user engagement patterns.

The cultural context also plays a critical role in shaping herd mentality. Different societies exhibit varying degrees of conformity based on historical, social, and cultural norms. For example, collectivist cultures may encourage conformity more than individualistic cultures, leading to distinct patterns in consumer behavior and workplace dynamics. Understanding these cultural dimensions is crucial for psychology students and analysts, as they can significantly influence how herd behavior manifests across diverse populations. This cultural lens allows for a deeper appreciation of the motivations behind collective actions in various settings.

Educational settings provide another context in which herd behavior can be observed and analyzed. Students often navigate social hierarchies and peer dynamics, which can influence their academic choices and social interactions. The findings suggest that educators need to be aware of these dynamics to create environments that encourage independent thinking while acknowledging the natural inclination towards conformity. By fostering a culture of critical thinking, educational institutions can mitigate the negative aspects of herd behavior, empowering students to make informed decisions rather than merely following the crowd.

Finally, the impact of technology on herd mentality is profound, with advancements in communication tools altering the way information is disseminated and consumed. The immediacy of digital communication can exacerbate the speed at which herd behavior develops, as seen in viral trends and social movements. Understanding this relationship is essential for both psychology students and social media analysts, as it highlights the need for strategies that address the rapid spread of misinformation and the potential for groupthink. By recognizing the psychological triggers behind herd behavior, stakeholders can better navigate the complexities of social influence in an increasingly interconnected world.

Implications for Future Research

The exploration of herd behavior has opened new avenues for research that can significantly enhance our understanding of social dynamics. Future studies could focus on the mechanisms that underlie herd mentality in various contexts, particularly in educational settings. Analyzing how groupthink influences student decision-making and learning outcomes can provide insights into effective teaching strategies. Researchers could investigate whether interventions that promote critical thinking can mitigate the negative effects of conformity in classrooms, thus contributing to a more nuanced understanding of how herding impacts academic performance.

In the realm of social media, the implications for future research are particularly pronounced. As platforms evolve, the ways in which information spreads and influences behavior continue to change. Understanding the psychological triggers that drive users to conform to social norms online can help explain phenomena such as viral trends and collective actions. Future studies could examine the role of algorithms in shaping user behavior, exploring how these digital environments either exacerbate or alleviate herd mentality. This research is critical, as it can inform strategies for responsible social media use and the development of tools that promote individual agency.

Moreover, the intersection of cultural factors and herd behavior presents a rich area for future inquiry. Different cultures exhibit varying degrees of collectivism and individualism, which influence how herd mentality manifests. Comparative studies examining herd behavior across diverse cultural contexts can reveal the extent to which cultural norms shape social influence. This line of research may also delve into how globalization affects local herd behaviors, leading to either homogenization or the preservation of distinct cultural practices in consumer behavior and workplace dynamics.

Understanding herd mentality in consumer behavior is another vital area for future research. As markets become increasingly saturated and consumers face overwhelming choices, the tendency to follow the crowd can have significant implications for marketing strategies. Researchers could investigate the psychological triggers that lead consumers to make decisions based on perceived social validation. This could include examining the role of influencer marketing and how social proof affects purchasing behavior. Insights gained from such studies can be instrumental for businesses seeking to harness the power of herd behavior effectively while remaining ethical in their practices.

Lastly, the impact of technology on herd mentality warrants further exploration. The rapid advancement of communication technologies has transformed the ways individuals interact and influence one another. Future research should investigate how virtual environments, such as online forums and gaming communities, cultivate new forms of herd behavior. By analyzing the dynamics within these spaces, researchers can uncover the psychological triggers that facilitate group cohesion and conformity. Understanding these mechanisms can help in designing interventions that promote healthier interactions in digital communities, thereby reducing the potential for harmful herd behavior.

Final Thoughts on Herd Behavior and Society

In examining the nuances of herd behavior, it becomes clear that this phenomenon is not merely an individual quirk but a reflection of deep-seated psychological mechanisms that govern social interactions. The tendency for individuals to conform to the actions or beliefs of a larger group can be traced back to evolutionary survival instincts. As social creatures, humans have historically benefited from group cohesion, which provided safety and resources. This instinctual drive continues to shape our behaviors in modern contexts, including consumer choices and workplace dynamics. Understanding these underlying motivations is crucial for psychology students and social media analysts alike, as it informs how we interpret collective behavior in various settings.

Social media has emerged as a powerful catalyst for herd behavior, amplifying the effects of conformity and social influence. Platforms such as Twitter, Facebook, and Instagram facilitate rapid dissemination of information, enabling trends to emerge almost instantaneously. This immediacy can create a bandwagon effect, where individuals feel compelled to join a popular movement or endorse a trending opinion, often without critical evaluation. For social media analysts, the challenge lies in discerning genuine engagement from herd-driven actions, which can skew perceptions of public sentiment and influence marketing strategies. Recognizing the psychological triggers behind these actions allows for more informed approaches to content creation and audience engagement.

In the realm of consumer behavior, herd mentality plays a pivotal role in decision-making processes. People are more likely to purchase products or services that they observe others endorsing, often prioritizing collective approval over personal preferences. This behavior is exacerbated by social proof, a psychological phenomenon where individuals look to others for cues on how to behave in uncertain situations. For students of psychology, this presents a fertile ground for exploring the intersection of human cognition and market dynamics. Understanding how social validation influences consumer choices can lead to more effective marketing strategies and a deeper comprehension of economic trends.

Workplace dynamics are also profoundly affected by herd behavior, as employees often conform to group norms and expectations, sometimes at the expense of individual creativity and critical thinking. This can lead to a culture of compliance where innovative ideas are stifled, and dissent is discouraged. For educators and organizational leaders, fostering an environment that values diverse perspectives and encourages constructive dissent is essential to combat the negative implications of herd mentality. By promoting psychological safety, organizations can harness the benefits of collaboration while mitigating the risks associated with groupthink.

Culturally, herd behavior manifests differently across societies, influenced by local norms, values, and technological advancements. In some cultures, collectivism may enhance the effects of herd mentality, while in others, individualism may promote dissenting viewpoints. As technology continues to reshape our social landscapes, the implications of herd behavior will likely evolve. For psychology students and analysts, the task ahead is to remain vigilant in observing these trends and their impacts on society. By deepening our understanding of herd behavior, we can better navigate the complexities of social influence, ultimately fostering environments that embrace both community and individuality.

Milton Keynes UK
Ingram Content Group UK Ltd.
UKHW032051201124
451474UK00005B/283

9 798330 550838